I ♥ RAMEN

TONI PATRICK

GIBBS SMITH
TO ENRICH AND INSPIRE HUMANKIND

First Edition
18 17 16 15 14   10 9 8 7 6 5 4 3 2 1

Text © 2014 Toni Patrick
Photographs © 2014 Susan Barnson Hayward

Published by
Gibbs Smith
P.O. Box 667
Layton, Utah 84041

1.800.835.4993 orders
www.gibbs-smith.com

Designed by Rita Sowins / Sowins Design
Corrine Miller Church: Food Stylist
Camille Whitehead: Food Stylist
Laura Hope Mason: Prop Stylist and Photographer's Assistant

Printed and bound in Hong Kong

Gibbs Smith books are printed on paper produced from sustainable PEFC-certified
forest/controlled wood source. Learn more at www.pefc.org.
Printed and bound in Hong Kong

Library of Congress Control Number: 2014939527

ISBN 978-1-4236-3807-0

CONTENTS

Introduction & Helpful Hints ... 7

Soups & Salads ... 9

Beef & Pork Mains ... 37

Chicken & Turkey Mains ... 73

Seafood Mains ... 93

Veggie Mains & Sides ... 103

Sweet on Ramen ... 119

Index ... 126

INTRODUCTION

I got the idea for a cookbook of recipes for using ramen noodles while in the dorms, cooking out of a hot pot. We would make the tuna noodle casserole and an egg drop soup. Since my mom, Georgie Patrick, and her friend Cyndi Duncan had already published some cookbooks, I made the joke that I should write one on ramen noodles. Six months later she called and said, "Get going!"

By then I was living in a house with five other students and abused them as test subjects. It was a great conversation topic every time I went out, because so many others were doing the same thing—just mixing ramen with whatever they had in the fridge or cabinet. My friends would call to tell me what their roommates had just eaten. We did a lot of experimenting, for instance, using milk instead of water; at one point we even tried it with beer. It was college, after all!

Today ramen noodles are still a cupboard staple for me because they are truly versatile, as the recipes in this book demonstrate. The possibilities are limited only by your imagination!

Helpful hints for cooking with packaged ramen noodles

1. Check ramen packaging for vegetarian or vegan manufacturers. Just because it is labeled as vegetable ramen does not mean animal products were not used in the manufacturing process.

2. Salt lovers beware. Taste before throwing in those extra dashes—the seasoning packets are salty.

3. Extra uses for ramen flavor packets:

» Add to water while preparing any noodle or rice for extra flavor.

» Use instead of bouillon—add 1 packet for every 2 cups of water.

» Use to flavor gravy—stir into pan drippings along with flour or whisk in water for use instead of stock.

» Shake and bake for potatoes.

- » Flavor cutlet, chop, or fish coating by mixing 1 packet per 2 tablespoons of flour.

- » Mix with bread crumbs for frying.

- » Season ground meat for burgers, meatballs, and meat loaf. Mix 1 packet per pound of ground meat.

- » Use as a seasoning rub for chicken, steaks, and pork chops.

4. To reduce fat and calories in recipes, substitute reduced-fat foods such as skim milk, light or fat-free sour cream, and light or fat-free cream cheese.

5. One clove garlic equals 1 teaspoon minced garlic. This is much more cost effective than using bottled minced garlic.

6. Two tablespoons dehydrated minced or chopped onion is equal to ¼ cup fresh minced onion.

7. One tablespoon dried herbs is equal to ¼ cup fresh herbs.

8. Fresh or frozen vegetables, steamed, can be substituted for canned vegetables.

9. As always, be creative! Most ingredients can be adjusted to your own liking.

10. To cook noodles, follow the directions on the package unless recipe says otherwise.

Soups & Salads

SLOW CHICKEN SOUP

Makes 6–8 servings

2 sweet potatoes, peeled and cubed
1 onion, chopped
1 (16-ounce) bag baby carrots
6 boneless, skinless chicken thighs, cubed
1/2 teaspoon dried thyme leaves
1/8 teaspoon pepper
6 cups water, divided
2 packages chicken ramen noodles, with seasoning packets
2 bay leaves

In a 4- to 5-quart slow cooker, layer the sweet potatoes, onion, carrots, and chicken. Sprinkle with thyme and pepper. In a small bowl, blend 1 cup water and seasoning packets. Pour over chicken and vegetables, add bay leaves and remaining water. Cover and cook on low for 7–9 hours or until vegetables and chicken are tender. Remove and discard bay leaves. Stir in noodles and cover. Cook on high 10–12 minutes or until noodles are tender, stirring once during cooking.

CURRIED CHICKEN SOUP

Makes 8–10 servings

2 large carrots, diced
2 large celery stalks, diced
1 small onion, chopped
3/4 cup butter or margarine
3/4 cup flour
2 packages chicken or vegetable ramen, crushed and with seasoning packets
1 teaspoon curry powder
3 (12-ounce) cans evaporated milk
2 cups water
2 cups chicken broth
3 cups cubed cooked chicken

In a large saucepan, sauté carrots, celery, and onion in butter until tender. Stir in the flour, seasoning packets, and curry until smooth. Gradually add milk. Bring to a boil, stirring regularly until thickened. Gradually add water and broth. Return to a boil and add chicken and noodles. Continue to boil for 3 minutes. Remove from heat and serve.

HAM & BLACK-EYED PEAS

Makes 4–6 servings

1 tablespoon vegetable oil
2 cups chopped collard greens
¼ cup chopped green onions, divided
1 clove garlic, chopped
6 cups water
2 packages pork ramen noodles, with seasoning packets
1 cup diced ham
1 (15-ounce) can black-eyed peas, drained and rinsed
2 tablespoons chopped cilantro

Add oil to a large saucepan over medium-high heat. When the oil is warm, add collard greens, half of the onions, and garlic. Stir-fry for 2 minutes. Don't overcook; the collards should still be bright green. Add water and seasoning packets and bring to a boil. Add noodles, ham, and black-eyed peas. Allow to simmer for 3 minutes. Portion and garnish with reserved onion and cilantro.

SPICY SHRIMP & NOODLE SOUP

Makes 6–8 servings

1 tablespoon lemon juice
¼ teaspoon chili powder
¼ teaspoon ground cumin
⅛ teaspoon pepper
1 pound ready-to-cook shrimp
6 cups water
2 packages oriental ramen noodles, with seasoning packets
2 cups salsa
1 (15-ounce) can black beans, rinsed and drained
1 (15-ounce) can corn, drained
1 green onion, sliced

In a medium bowl, combine lemon juice, chili powder, cumin, and pepper; add shrimp and toss to coat. Let stand 20 minutes.

In a large saucepan bring the water and seasoning packets to boil. Add noodles, shrimp, salsa, beans, corn, and onion; heat though until shrimp turn pink, about 3 minutes.

SOUTH OF THE BORDER RAMEN SOUP

Makes 2–4 servings

3 cups water
1 lime, juiced
4 tablespoons chili powder
1 teaspoon garlic powder
Dash of hot sauce
¼ teaspoon chopped cilantro
2 packages chicken ramen noodles, with seasoning packets
1 chicken breast, cooked and cubed
1 (16-ounce) can corn, drained
1 (16-ounce) can black beans, drained and rinsed
1 medium avocado, diced
¼ cup sour cream
Tortilla chips, crushed

In a large saucepan add water, lime juice, chili powder, garlic, hot sauce, cilantro, and seasoning packets. Bring to a boil over medium heat. Add noodles, chicken, corn, and beans. Allow to cook for 3 minutes. Portion into bowls and top with avocado, sour cream, and tortilla chips.

MISO & VEGGIE RAMEN SOUP

Makes 4–6 servings

2 teaspoons olive oil
1 teaspoon minced fresh ginger
1 clove garlic, minced
2 ounces ground pork
2 carrots, cut into thin strips
1 cup bean sprouts, rinsed
1 cup chopped cabbage
4 cups water
2 packages chicken ramen noodles, with seasoning packets
1 teaspoon sugar
2 teaspoons light soy sauce
4 tablespoons miso
$\frac{1}{2}$ teaspoon sesame oil

Heat olive oil in a large saucepan or a wok and cook the ginger, garlic, and pork on medium heat until pork is no longer pink. Add carrots, sprouts, and cabbage and sauté for 2 minutes, stirring. Add the water, seasoning packets, sugar, and soy sauce; mix and bring to a boil. Add noodles and allow to simmer for 3 minutes. Turn heat down to low and melt miso in the soup. Add sesame oil and remove from heat.

CHUNKY NOODLE SALAD

Makes 2–4 servings

2 packages chicken ramen noodles, with seasoning packets
2 teaspoons sesame oil
3 tablespoons lemon juice
1/3 cup vegetable oil
2 teaspoons sugar
1 cup halved red and/or green seedless grapes
1/2 cup diced red and/or green apple
1/2 cup diced pineapple chunks
3 tablespoons chopped green onion
8 ounces smoked turkey breast, cut into strips
1/4 cup walnut pieces

Cook noodles in water according to package directions and drain. Rinse with cold water. Add sesame oil and refrigerate.

For dressing, combine lemon juice, vegetable oil, seasoning packets, and sugar. Pour over noodles then add remaining ingredients. Toss to coat.

TOSSED MANDARIN SALAD

Makes 6–8 servings

2 packages ramen noodles, any flavor, crushed
1 cup peanuts, chopped
1 (16-ounce) package coleslaw mix
1 bunch green onions, sliced
1 small red bell pepper, sliced
1 (15-ounce) can mandarin orange segments, drained
½ cup sugar
½ cup vegetable oil
¼ cup cider vinegar
1 tablespoon soy sauce

Preheat oven to 350 degrees.

Place the noodles and peanuts on a baking sheet and toast until golden brown, about 15 minutes. Remove from oven and allow to cool.

In a large bowl, combine coleslaw, onions, bell pepper, oranges, noodles, and peanuts; toss. In a small bowl, mix the sugar, oil, vinegar, and soy sauce until well combined. Pour over the salad and toss to coat.

CRUNCHY FRUIT SALAD

Makes 4-6 servings

2 large oranges, peeled and diced
1 large pear, diced
1 large apple, diced
5 tablespoons brown sugar
1 package ramen noodles, any flavor, crushed

In a large bowl, combine the fruit and brown sugar. Mix well and allow it to sit for 5 minutes; toss. Just before serving, add crushed noodles and toss again.

ANTIPASTO SALAD

Makes 2–4 servings

2 packages ramen noodles, any flavor
³/₄ cup cubed pepperoni
¹/₂ cup sliced black olives
¹/₄ cup sliced onion
Italian dressing

Cook noodles in water according to package directions and drain. Add pepperoni, olives, and onion. Drizzle desired amount of dressing over top and toss to coat.

NUTTY BROCCOLI SLAW

Makes 6 servings

²/₃ cup vegetable oil
¹/₃ cup white vinegar
¹/₄ cup sugar
1 package chicken ramen noodles, crushed and with seasoning packet
1 (16-ounce) package broccoli coleslaw
2 bunches green onions, thinly sliced
³/₄ cup dried cranberries
¹/₂ cup sliced almonds
¹/₂ cup sunflower seeds

In a small bowl, combine oil, vinegar, sugar, and seasoning packet to make the dressing. Mix until sugar dissolves and chill for at least 30 minutes.

Combine broccoli coleslaw, onions, and cranberries in a large bowl. In a medium bowl, combine the almonds, noodles, and sunflower seeds. When ready to serve, combine all ingredients together and toss.

TACO SALAD

Makes 2–4 servings

2 packages beef ramen noodles, with seasoning packets
1 pound ground beef, browned and drained
1 large tomato, chopped
¾ cup chopped onion
2 cups grated cheddar cheese
Thousand Island dressing or salsa

Cook noodles in water according to package directions and drain. In a medium bowl, stir 1 seasoning packet into cooked beef. Add tomato, onion, and cheese. Spoon mixture over warm noodles and drizzle with dressing or salsa.

QUICK CHICKEN SALAD

Makes 6–8 servings

2 boneless, skinless chicken breast halves, cooked and diced
$\frac{1}{2}$ cup slivered or sliced almonds
2 green onions, sliced
1 tablespoon sugar
2 tablespoons sesame seeds
1 package chicken ramen noodles, crushed and with seasoning packet
$\frac{1}{2}$ medium head lettuce, shredded
$\frac{1}{2}$ cup vegetable oil
3 tablespoons white vinegar

In a large bowl, combine the chicken, almonds, onions, sugar, sesame seeds, noodles, and lettuce.

In a small bowl, combine the oil, seasoning packet, and vinegar. Pour dressing over salad and toss to coat. Let stand overnight in refrigerator.

ORIENTAL CHICKEN SALAD

Makes 6 servings

³/₄ cup plus 3 tablespoons vegetable oil, divided
4 ¹/₂ tablespoons seasoned rice vinegar
4 ¹/₂ tablespoons sugar
2 packages oriental ramen noodles, finely crushed and with seasoning packets
1 cup slivered almonds
1 head cabbage, shredded
1 bunch green onions, finely chopped
2 cups cooked and diced chicken breasts
3 tablespoons sunflower seeds

In a small bowl, mix ³/₄ cup oil, vinegar, sugar, and 1 seasoning packet to make the dressing.

In a medium frying pan, add remaining oil and noodles. Cook over medium heat until lightly brown. Add almonds and continue to cook until almonds are toasted. Remove from pan and set aside.

Combine cabbage, onions, chicken, and sunflower seeds in a large bowl. Add the noodle mixture and toss. Add dressing and toss to coat.

TOFU & CABBAGE TOSS

Makes 4–6 servings

2 cups cubed tofu
2 tablespoons soy sauce
¼ teaspoon garlic powder
¼ teaspoon onion powder
2 tablespoons sugar
3 tablespoons white vinegar
⅛ cup, plus 1 tablespoon sesame oil, divided
⅛ cup olive oil
1 package ramen noodles, any flavor, crushed
3 tablespoons sesame seeds
¼ cup slivered almonds
4 green onions, thinly sliced
1 red bell pepper, diced
½ head cabbage, shredded

Preheat oven to 350 degrees.

Place tofu on several paper towels, cover with another paper towel, and press to remove liquid.

In a small bowl, whisk the soy sauce, garlic powder, onion powder, sugar, vinegar, ⅛ cup sesame oil, and olive oil. Place in a ziplock bag and add tofu. Flip to distribute marinade. Allow to sit 5 minutes, shaking regularly.

In a small bowl, add crushed noodles, sesame seeds, almonds, and remaining sesame oil; toss to coat. Spread the mixture onto a baking sheet and bake for 10 minutes. Stir and bake 5 minutes more, or until the noodles are golden brown. Allow to cool completely.

In a large bowl, combine the onions, bell pepper, and cabbage. Add toasted mixture and tofu with marinade; toss to coat.

TANGERINE CHICKEN SALAD

Makes 6–8 servings

1 (15-ounce) can tangerines or mandarin oranges, juice reserved
¼ cup cider vinegar
2 tablespoons sugar
2 tablespoons soy sauce
2 teaspoons plus 1 tablespoon sesame oil, divided
2 packages chicken ramen noodles, crushed
2 tablespoons sesame seeds
½ cup slivered almonds
½ head red or green cabbage, sliced
1 cup shredded carrots
1 bunch green onions, chopped
1 head lettuce, sliced
1 chicken breast, cooked and finely diced

Preheat oven to 350 degrees.

In a small bowl, whisk together the reserved juice, vinegar, sugar, soy sauce, and 2 teaspoons sesame oil to make the dressing; set aside. In a medium bowl, toss the noodles, sesame seeds, almonds, and remaining sesame oil. Spread the mixture onto a baking sheet and bake for 10 minutes. Stir and bake 5 minutes more, or until the noodles are golden brown. Remove from oven and allow to cool completely.

In a large serving bowl, combine the cabbage, carrots, onions, and lettuce. Add the toasted noodle mixture, tangerines, chicken, and dressing; toss to coat.

CHICKEN FAJITA RAMEN SALAD

Makes 6 servings

1 package spicy ramen noodles, crushed and with seasoning packet
2 boneless, skinless chicken breasts
3 tablespoons vegetable oil, divided
1 small onion, sliced
1 small red bell pepper, sliced
1 small green bell pepper, sliced
1 large tomato, diced
2 limes, juiced
1 teaspoon dried cilantro
2 tablespoons soy sauce
$1/2$ tablespoon cayenne pepper
1 teaspoon sugar

Lightly sprinkle seasoning packet on both sides of chicken breasts (using about a fourth of the packet in all). Place 2 tablespoons oil in a large frying pan over medium heat. Brown each side of chicken breasts, then cover and cook until done. Cut into strips and place in a large bowl. Sauté the onion and bell peppers in the pan until tender. Add to chicken, along with noodles and tomato; toss to mix.

In a small bowl, whisk together the lime juice, cilantro, soy sauce, cayenne pepper, sugar, remaining oil, and remaining seasoning from packet. Drizzle over chicken mixture and toss. Can be served immediately or chilled and served cold.

THREE SPROUT SALAD

Makes 4–6 servings

6 cups water
2 packages ramen noodles, any flavor
2/3 cup alfalfa sprouts
3 tablespoons sesame seeds
1/4 cup red wine vinegar
2 tablespoons soy sauce
2 tablespoons sesame oil
1 1/2 tablespoons sugar
1 teaspoon Chinese red chili sauce
1/3 cup sliced green onions
2 tablespoons minced fresh gingerroot
2 cups bean sprouts
1/2 cup radish sprouts

In a large saucepan, bring water to a boil. Add noodles and cook for 3 minutes; drain and set aside. Pull alfalfa sprouts apart; set aside.

In a small ungreased frying pan over high heat, toast the sesame seeds until golden, about 4 minutes. Remove from pan and set aside.

In a small bowl, combine the vinegar, soy sauce, sesame oil, sugar, chili sauce, onions, and ginger. Mix well and add to noodles; toss to coat and refrigerate for at least 1 hour.

Toss noodles with sprouts and seeds.

POLISH RAMEN SALAD

Makes 6–8 servings

3 teaspoons mayonnaise
1 cup plain yogurt
2 teaspoons paprika
3 packages chicken ramen noodles, crushed and with seasoning packets
2 tomatoes, diced
1 cucumber, diced
1 (15-ounce) can corn, drained
1 (12.5-ounce) can kidney beans, rinsed and drained

In a large bowl, whisk together the mayonnaise, yogurt, paprika, and 1 seasoning packet. Add noodles and toss to coat. Add the tomatoes, cucumber, corn, and beans. Toss to coat and refrigerate for at least 1 hour.

Beef & Pork Mains

RAMEN ROLLED STEAK

Makes 6–8 servings

1½ pounds flank steak
1 package beef ramen noodles, crushed and with seasoning packet
Pepper
1 egg
1 tablespoon water
1 tablespoon flour
2 tablespoons steak sauce

Preheat oven to 350 degrees.

Lay a large piece of plastic wrap on a cutting board. One at a time, set each piece of steak on the plastic wrap and fold over to cover. Pound the steak to about ½-inch thickness. Sprinkle seasoning packet and pepper to taste on both sides of the steaks and rub in.

In small bowl, beat the egg and water. Whisk in flour until there are no lumps. Spread the mixture on one side of each of the pounded steaks. Sprinkle evenly with the crushed noodles. Roll up and pin each roll with at least 4 toothpicks. Place each roll in a mini loaf pan or place rolls in a baking dish that has been prepared with nonstick cooking spray. Bake for 30–35 minutes, uncovered. Rub rolled steak with steak sauce, and bake for 10 minutes more. Remove from oven and let cool for about 10 minutes before cutting. Slice between toothpicks and serve.

YATSOBI

Makes 4–6 servings

1 pound lean ground beef
6 slices bacon
1 medium red onion, diced
3 tablespoons minced garlic
3 tablespoons soy sauce
3 carrots, cut into thin strips
1 medium cabbage, chopped
1 red bell pepper, diced
4 cups water
2 packages ramen noodles, any flavor
Splash olive oil
3 cups bean sprouts

In a large frying pan, brown the ground beef; drain and set aside. In the same pan, fry the bacon until crispy; drain on paper towels and reserve 2 tablespoons of the bacon fat. Stir the onion and garlic into the fat and cook for 3–4 minutes or until onions are soft. Add the soy sauce and carrots and cook for 2–3 minutes. Add cabbage and bell pepper and stir-fry on medium heat for 5–6 minutes, or until vegetables are tender-crisp. Add ground beef and bacon to the vegetable mixture and cook on medium heat for 2–3 minutes, or until meat is heated through.

In a large saucepan, bring water to a boil. Add noodles and cook for 3 minutes; drain and toss with olive oil to keep from sticking together.

Add bean sprouts to meat and vegetable mixture and cook for 3 minutes, stirring frequently. Divide noodles among individual plates, then spoon meat and vegetable mixture over the top.

SLOW COOKER BEEF & NOODLES

Makes 10–14 servings

2 pounds beef roast
14 cups water, divided
6 packages beef ramen noodles, with seasoning packets
2 large white onions, diced

Place roast in a 4-quart slow cooker with 1 cup water on low heat and allow to cook overnight or for 8–9 hours. Shred the meat and add all seasoning packets, onion, and 1 cup water. Allow to cook, on low, another 1–2 hours.

About 15 minutes before serving, bring remaining water to a boil in a large saucepan. Add noodles and cook for 3 minutes. Drain, place in a large serving bowl, and mix in the beef.

BEEF RAMENOFF

Makes 2 servings

½ pound beef strips
2 cups sour cream
1 tablespoon chopped chives
1 teaspoon salt
⅛ teaspoon pepper
1 clove garlic, crushed
½ cup grated Parmesan cheese, divided
1 package ramen noodles, any flavor
2 tablespoons butter or margarine

In a large frying pan, brown beef until cooked through. Add sour cream, chives, salt, pepper, garlic, and ¼ cup Parmesan cheese. Simmer over low heat until sour cream is melted. Stir all together.

Cook noodles in water according to package directions and drain. Stir butter into warm noodles until melted. Fold in beef mixture. Sprinkle with remaining cheese.

STUFFED BELL PEPPERS

Makes 6 servings

3 green bell peppers
1 (14.5-ounce) can diced tomatoes, divided
1 (8-ounce) can tomato sauce, divided
1 tablespoon olive oil
1 small onion, diced
4 tablespoons minced garlic
1 pound ground beef
1 package beef ramen noodles, finely crushed, and with seasoning packet
½ cup grated Monterey Jack cheese

Preheat oven to 375 degrees.

Cut bell peppers in half, crosswise. Remove seeds and place on paper towels to drain.

In a medium mixing bowl, combine a third of the tomatoes and half the tomato sauce and set aside.

Add the olive oil to a large frying pan. Heat on medium low and add the onion and garlic. Sauté for 4–5 minutes or until soft. Add the beef and seasoning packet, mix well, and continue to cook until beef has browned. Remove from heat. Add the noodles, remaining tomatoes, and remaining tomato sauce; mix well.

Place the bell peppers as bowls in a 9 x 13-inch glass casserole dish and fill with beef mixture. Top with the tomato sauce mixture. Cover with foil and bake for about 1 hour, or until peppers are tender. Uncover and bake 10 minutes more. Sprinkle with cheese and bake for 5 minutes.

CREAMY BEEF & BROCCOLI NOODLES

Makes 2 servings

3/4 pound beef sirloin, cubed
1/2 teaspoon garlic powder
1 onion, cut into wedges
2 cups broccoli pieces
1 (10.75-ounce) can cream of broccoli soup, condensed
1/4 cup water
1 tablespoon soy sauce
2 packages beef ramen noodles, with seasoning packets

In a large frying pan, brown beef with garlic powder until done. Stir in onion and broccoli. Cook over medium heat until vegetables are tender. Add soup, water, and soy sauce. Simmer 10 minutes.

Cook noodles in water according to package directions and drain. Add seasoning packets. Serve beef mixture over warm noodles.

BEEF PROVENÇALE

Makes 2 servings

1 pound beef strips
2 tablespoons butter or margarine
1 onion, sliced
2 tablespoons flour
1 cup water mixed with seasoning packet
1 tomato, chopped
1 (4-ounce) can sliced mushrooms, drained
1 teaspoon garlic powder
1 package beef ramen noodles, with seasoning packet

In a large frying pan, brown beef until done; drain and set aside.

In a large saucepan, heat butter until golden brown. Add onion and cook until tender, then discard onion. Stir in flour, over low heat, until it is brown. Remove from heat. Add water mixture and heat to boiling, stirring constantly for 1 minute. Gently stir in tomato, mushrooms, and garlic powder.

Cook noodles in water according to package directions and drain. Top warm noodles with beef and sauce.

CHEDDAR BEEF CASSEROLE

Makes 2–4 servings

2 packages beef ramen noodles, with seasoning packets
1 pound ground beef
1/2 cup sliced celery
1/4 cup chopped green bell pepper
1/2 cup chopped onion
3 cups grated cheddar cheese
2 cups corn
1 (6-ounce) can tomato paste
1/2 cup water

Preheat oven to 350 degrees.

Cook noodles in water according to package directions; drain and set aside.

In a large frying pan, brown beef with celery, pepper, and onion; drain and set aside. In a 2-quart casserole dish, mix remaining ingredients with 1 seasoning packet. Add beef mixture and noodles. Cover and bake 15–20 minutes.

BEEFY MUSHROOM NOODLES

Makes 2–4 servings

2 packages beef ramen noodles, with seasoning packets
1¹⁄₂ pounds beef strips
¹⁄₄ cup butter or margarine
2 (4-ounce) cans sliced mushrooms, drained
¹⁄₄ cup flour
2 cups water mixed with seasoning packets
Worcestershire sauce

Cook noodles in water according to package directions and drain.

In a large frying pan, brown beef until cooked through; drain.

In a small saucepan, melt butter over low heat. Stir in mushrooms and brown slowly. Add flour and cook, stirring, until deep brown. Add water mixture. Heat to boiling and stir 1 minute. Add Worcestershire sauce to taste. Top warm noodles with beef and sauce.

BEEF & BROCCOLI STIR-FRY

Makes 2–4 servings

1 pound beef steak strips
1 tablespoon oil
2 cups broccoli pieces
1 cup green onions, cut into strips
2 tablespoons soy sauce
¼ teaspoon crushed red pepper
2 packages beef ramen noodles, with seasoning packets

In a large frying pan, brown beef until cooked through; drain. Add oil, 1 seasoning packet, broccoli, and onions. Stir-fry 5 minutes. Add soy sauce and red pepper. Simmer 5 minutes more.

Cook noodles in water according to package directions and drain. Serve beef mixture over warm noodles.

BEEF SUKIYAKI

Makes 2–4 servings

1 pound stir-fry beef
2 tablespoons vegetable oil
½ cup water mixed with half of 1 seasoning packet
2 tablespoons sugar
½ cup soy sauce
1 (4-ounce) can sliced mushrooms, drained
½ cup sliced green onions
1 cup sliced onion
1 celery stalk, sliced
1 small can bamboo shoots
3 cups fresh spinach
2 packages beef ramen noodles, with seasoning packets

In a large frying pan, brown beef in oil until cooked through; push to one side of the pan. Stir in water, sugar, and soy sauce. Add remaining ingredients except noodles and cook until tender. Cover and simmer 5 minutes. Stir together.

Cook noodles in water according to package directions and drain. Add seasoning packets. Serve beef mixture over warm noodles.

BEEF & CHESTNUT CASSEROLE

Makes 4–6 servings

1 pound ground beef
2 packages beef ramen noodles, with seasoning packets
1 medium onion, chopped
3 cups water
1 (10.5-ounce) can cream of mushroom soup, condensed
1 (10.5-ounce) can cream of celery soup, condensed
1 (5-ounce) can sliced water chestnuts
½ cup milk
1 cup grated cheddar cheese, divided

Preheat oven to 350 degrees.

In a large frying pan, brown the ground beef with seasoning packets and onion. In a medium saucepan, bring water to a boil and add the noodles; cook for 3 minutes and then drain. When beef is browned, add noodles, soups, water chestnuts, milk, and ½ cup cheese. Pour into an 8 x 8-inch glass baking dish that has been prepared with nonstick cooking spray and top with remaining cheese. Bake uncovered for 20–25 minutes.

BEEFY CHILI NOODLES

Makes 2–4 servings

1 pound ground beef
2 packages beef ramen noodles, with seasoning packets
2 (4-ounce) cans sliced mushrooms, drained
1/2 cup chopped onion
1/2 cup chopped tomato
1 (15-ounce) can kidney beans, rinsed and drained
1/4 teaspoon chili powder
1 cup water

In a large frying pan, brown beef until done; drain. Add remaining ingredients and 1 seasoning packet. Simmer 10 minutes over medium heat or until noodles are done.

CHEESEBURGER RAMEN

Makes 2 servings

½ pound ground beef
1 package beef ramen noodles, with seasoning packet
1 cup grated cheddar cheese
1 tomato, diced (optional)

In a medium frying pan, brown beef until done; drain. Season to taste with about half of the seasoning packet.

Cook noodles in water according to package directions and drain. Add beef and cheese to noodles and stir until cheese is melted. Add tomatoes, if desired.

ORIENTAL HOT DOGS

Makes 1–2 servings

4 cups water
2 packages oriental ramen noodles, with seasoning packets
¼ cup sliced yellow onion
1 zucchini, diagonally sliced
2 hot dogs, diagonally sliced
¼ cup mustard greens
Chives, for garnish

In a large saucepan, bring water to a boil. Add the seasoning packets, onion, and zucchini and reduce to medium heat. Allow to simmer for 1 minute. Add hot dogs and simmer for 1 minute. Add noodles and simmer for 2 minutes. Add mustard greens and simmer for 1 minute more. Serve topped with chives.

CHEESY BACON NOODLES

Makes 2–4 servings

2 packages ramen noodles, any flavor
2 cups grated cheddar cheese
$1/2$–1 cup bacon, cooked and crumbled
Salt and pepper

Cook noodles in water according to package directions and drain. Add cheese immediately and stir until melted. Stir in bacon and season to taste with salt and pepper.

PORK CHOPS & RAMEN

Makes 4 servings

4 pork chops
1 teaspoon oil
1/2 cup sliced onion
1 (10.75-ounce) can cream of celery soup, condensed
1/2 cup water
2 packages pork ramen noodles, with seasoning packets

In a large frying pan over medium heat, brown pork chops in oil 5 minutes per side, or until done, and drain. Add onion, soup, and water. Simmer over low heat 10 minutes.

Cook noodles in water according to package directions and drain. Add seasoning packets. Serve pork chops and sauce over warm noodles.

HUNGARIAN GOULASH À LA RAMEN

Makes 2 servings

1 package ramen noodles, any flavor
1/2 pound pork strips
1 (8-ounce) can tomato sauce
1/4 cup onion, thinly sliced
1 teaspoon paprika
1/3 cup sour cream

Cook noodles in water according to package directions and drain.

In a large frying pan, brown pork until done. Add tomato sauce, onion, paprika, and noodles. Cook over low heat until onion is tender. Stir in noodles. Remove from heat and add sour cream.

SAUCY CHOPS & PEPPERS

Makes 2 servings

2 pork chops
1/4 cup chopped red bell pepper
1/4 cup chopped green bell pepper
2 tablespoons chopped onion
1 package pork ramen noodles, with seasoning packet
2 tablespoons butter or margarine
2 tablespoons flour
1 cup water mixed with seasoning packet
1 tablespoon vinegar
1/4 teaspoon tarragon leaves
1/4 teaspoon thyme leaves

In a medium frying pan, brown pork chops until done and then remove. Sauté peppers and onion in drippings until tender.

Cook noodles in water according to package directions and drain.

In a small saucepan, heat butter over low heat until light brown. Add flour, stirring until deep brown. Remove from heat. Add remaining ingredients plus sautéed peppers and onion. Heat to boiling and stir 1 minute. Top warm noodles with pork chops and sauce.

TROPICAL RAMEN

Makes 2 servings

2 packages ramen noodles, any flavor
2 cups fully-cooked ham, cut into strips
1 cup pineapple chunks
1 cup crispy Chinese noodles
1 stalk celery, sliced

Cook noodles in water according to package directions and drain. Rinse with cold water.

Stir in ham, pineapple, crispy noodles, and celery.

BROCCOLI, MUSHROOM & HAM CASSEROLE

Makes 6–8 servings

4 cups water
2 packages chicken ramen noodles, with seasoning packets
2 large heads broccoli, cut into bite-size pieces
2 cups plain yogurt
4 eggs
1 (12-ounce) package fresh mushrooms, washed and sliced
2 cups cooked diced ham
2 cups grated mild cheddar cheese
1 medium onion, diced

Preheat oven to 350 degrees.

Prepare a 12 x 17-inch casserole dish with nonstick cooking spray.

In a medium saucepan, bring water to a boil. Add noodles and cook for 3 minutes; drain.

In a large microwave-safe bowl, add the broccoli and fill with water until broccoli is completely covered. Microwave on high for 6 minutes; drain.

In a large bowl, combine the yogurt, eggs, and seasoning packets; mix thoroughly. Add the broccoli, mushrooms, ham, cheese, onion, and noodles then toss together to evenly coat. Pour into prepared dish and bake for 1 hour, or until center is bubbly. Allow to set for 15 minutes before serving.

SPICY SAUSAGE RAMEN

Makes 1–2 servings

2–3 spicy Italian sausage links
¼ cup diced onion
½ cup diced green bell pepper
1 tablespoon minced garlic
2 cups water
1 package chili ramen noodles, with seasoning packet
1 (14.5-ounce) can stewed tomatoes

Poke each sausage with a fork to allow grease to escape. In a large frying pan, cook the sausage over medium heat. Remove sausage and then slice and set aside. Sauté the onion, bell pepper, and garlic in the pan with the grease from the sausage until tender.

In a large saucepan, combine water, flavor packet, and tomatoes. Bring to a boil and add noodles, sausage, and vegetables. Cook for 3 minutes.

GINGERED PORK & SNOW PEAS

Makes 4–6 servings

1 pound boneless pork shoulder, cut into 1-inch pieces
2 packages chicken ramen noodles, crumbled and with seasoning packets
1 teaspoon grated gingerroot
3 cups water
1 cup halved fresh snow pea pods
¼ cup sliced green onion
1 tablespoon soy sauce
2 teaspoons cornstarch

In 3½- to 4-quart slow cooker, combine the pork, seasoning packets, gingerroot and water; mix. Cover and cook on low heat for 6–8 hours.

About 30 minutes before serving, add the noodles, pea pods, and onion; mix. Turn heat setting to high; cover and cook for 10 minutes more or just until vegetables are tender-crisp.

In a small bowl, blend the soy sauce and cornstarch until smooth. Stir into pork mixture and cook for 5 minutes or until sauce is slightly thickened.

BREAKFAST RAMEN

Makes 1–2 servings

2 cups water
1 package chicken ramen noodles
2 eggs
¼ cup grated cheddar cheese
4 slices bacon, chopped
4 large mushrooms, diced
1 small tomato, diced

In a small saucepan, boil water. Add noodles and cook for 3 minutes; drain and place in a large bowl. Beat eggs and pour over noodles; toss. Add cheese and toss again.

In a large frying pan over medium heat, cook bacon pieces until bacon starts to crisp, stirring regularly to keep pieces separated. Add mushrooms and sauté for 1 minute. Add tomato and continue to cook until bacon is done. Add noodles and toss until evenly distributed. Cook over medium heat for 3–4 minutes stirring to ensure all the egg has been cooked completely. Noodles will begin to brown.

BACON-FRIED RAMEN

Makes 1-2 servings

4 slices raw bacon, cut into ¼-inch pieces
3 cups water
2 packages ramen noodles, any flavor
Salt and pepper
Pinch of red pepper flakes
1 teaspoon soy sauce
1 egg

Place bacon into a large nonstick frying pan and let cook slowly on medium-low heat.

In a medium saucepan, bring water to a boil. Add noodles and cook for 3 minutes. Quickly drain the noodles completely and pour into a bowl of ice cold water to stop the cooking process. Stir the noodles with your hands until they are cold.

Once the bacon has finished cooking, drain the chilled noodles and combine with the bacon in the pan. Turn the stove up to medium-high heat. Season noodles and bacon with salt and pepper to taste, red pepper flakes, and soy sauce. Continue to cook for 2-3 minutes. Move noodles to one side of the pan. Crack the egg into open side of pan, mixing the egg in the pan and let it cook for 1-2 minutes. Cut up the egg and stir in with bacon and noodles. Continue cooking and turning for 3-4 more minutes.

Chicken & Turkey Mains

CHICKEN BROCCOLI BAKE

Makes 6–8 servings

3 tablespoons butter or margarine
1 package chicken ramen noodles, crushed
1 (16-ounce) bag frozen chopped broccoli
4 chicken breasts, cooked and diced
1 box broccoli and cheese rice mix, cooked according to package directions
1 (4-ounce) can sliced mushrooms, drained
1 cup sour cream
1 cup grated cheddar cheese
1 (10.5-ounce) can cream of mushroom soup, condensed
$1/2$ cup milk
1 tablespoon Worcestershire sauce
Dash of cayenne pepper

Preheat oven to 350 degrees.

Prepare a 9 x 13-inch glass casserole dish with nonstick cooking spray.

In a medium frying pan, melt the butter over medium heat, add noodles, and stir to coat with butter. Cook, stirring until noodles are lightly browned. Set aside for topping.

In a large microwave-safe bowl, add the broccoli and fill with water until broccoli is completely covered. Microwave on high for 6 minutes; drain. Combine with remaining ingredients in a large bowl, mixing well and pour into the casserole dish. Sprinkle noodles on top of casserole and bake for 18–20 minutes, or until heated through and cheese is melted.

CHEESY CHICKEN DIVAN

Makes 2–4 servings

2 cups fresh broccoli pieces
2–4 boneless, skinless chicken breasts, cut into chunks
2 packages chicken ramen noodles
1 (10.75-ounce) can cream of chicken soup, condensed
¾ cup mayonnaise
1 teaspoon mild curry powder
Salt and pepper
1 cup grated cheddar cheese

Preheat oven to 350 degrees.

Place broccoli in a medium saucepan and cover with water. Cook over medium heat until broccoli is tender; drain and spread in a lightly greased 9 x 9-inch casserole dish.

In a large frying pan, brown chicken until done. Spread chicken over broccoli.

Cook noodles in water according to package directions and drain. Spread noodles over broccoli and chicken.

Mix together soup, mayonnaise, curry powder, and salt and pepper to taste. Spoon mixture over broccoli, chicken, and noodles; sprinkle with cheese and bake 30 minutes.

HERBED CHICKEN

4 chicken breasts, cut into strips
1 tablespoon butter or margarine
$\frac{1}{2}$ cup diced carrots
$\frac{1}{4}$ cup diced onion
2 cups water
2 packages chicken ramen noodles, lightly crushed, with seasoning packets
Dash of dried marjoram
Dash of dried thyme
Pinch of dried rosemary
Pinch of rubbed sage

In a large frying pan, sauté the chicken in butter over medium heat until lightly brown. Add the carrots and onion; sauté until tender. Add water, 1 seasoning packet, and spices. Increase the heat and bring to a boil. Add noodles and continue to boil until water evaporates, stirring often.

HOT & SOUR RAMEN

Makes 1–2 servings

2 1/2 cups water, divided
1 package oriental ramen noodles, lightly crushed, with seasoning packet
1/2 teaspoon lemon juice
1 chicken breast, cooked and diced
1/4 cup frozen peas
1/4 cup frozen corn
1 teaspoon hot oil or Mongolian Fire Oil
1 tablespoon soy sauce
1 tablespoon cornstarch
2 eggs, beaten

In a large saucepan bring 2 cups of water to a boil. Add seasoning packet, lemon juice, chicken, peas, corn, hot oil, and soy sauce and cook for 3 minutes. Add noodles and continue to cook for 3 minutes more.

Mix cornstarch in remaining water. Slowly add to pan while stirring constantly. Let cook another minute or until mixture thickens. Slowly add the eggs, stirring constantly.

CHEESY CHICKEN CASSEROLE

Makes 2 servings

¼ cup chopped onion
2 tablespoons butter or margarine
1 (10.75-ounce) can cream of chicken soup, condensed
½ cup milk
1 package chicken ramen noodles, with seasoning packet
1 cup grated sharp cheddar cheese
1 small can white chicken chunks, drained

Preheat oven to 350 degrees.

In a small saucepan, sauté onion in butter until tender. Add soup, milk, and a little less than half of the seasoning packet. Stir until smooth.

Cook noodles in water according to package directions and drain. Add cheese, chicken, and soup mixture. Stir until cheese is melted. Pour into a 1-quart casserole dish that has been prepared with nonstick spray and bake 30 minutes.

CHICKEN 'N' ASPARAGUS

Makes 4 servings

4 boneless, skinless chicken breasts
2 packages chicken ramen noodles, with seasoning packets
2 (10.75-ounce) cans cream of asparagus or mushroom soup, condensed
1 cup milk
½ pound fresh asparagus, cut into 1-inch pieces
1 cup grated cheddar cheese

In a large frying pan, brown chicken until done. Add remaining ingredients, except cheese and 1 seasoning packet. Simmer over low heat 10 minutes, or until noodles are done. Sprinkle with cheese before serving.

HONEY GRILLED CHICKEN

Makes 3–6 servings

1 tablespoon creamy peanut butter
½ teaspoon red pepper flakes
¼ teaspoon ground ginger
1 teaspoon garlic powder
¼ cup honey
⅓ cup rice vinegar
2 tablespoons soy sauce
1 tablespoon sesame oil

2 tablespoons vegetable oil
3 boneless, skinless chicken breasts
3 cups water
2 medium carrots, sliced
2 cups broccoli florets
1 medium red bell pepper, sliced
1 package ramen noodles, any flavor
2 green onions, thinly sliced

Preheat the grill. In a medium bowl, combine peanut butter, red pepper flakes, ginger, garlic, honey, rice vinegar, soy sauce, and oils; stir to blend. Put 4 tablespoons of sauce in a ziplock bag for marinating; set aside remaining sauce. Place chicken in marinade in bag; seal and shake to coat. Refrigerate for at least 30 minutes or overnight.

In a large saucepan, bring water to a boil. Add carrots, broccoli, and bell pepper and cook over high heat until water comes to a rolling boil. Reduce heat to medium, add noodles and allow to cook for 3 minutes; drain. In a large bowl, combine the noodles and vegetables with the remaining sauce and onions. Toss to coat and cover with plastic wrap.

Grill chicken breasts over medium-hot coals for about 10 minutes, 5 minutes on each side or until done and juices run clear. Remove from grill and slice. Serve noodles topped with chicken slices.

CHICKEN ALFREDO

Makes 2 servings

2 boneless, skinless chicken breasts, cut into strips
2 packages ramen noodles, any flavor
1 cup butter or margarine
1 cup cream
2 cups grated Parmesan cheese
2 tablespoons parsley flakes
1/2 teaspoon salt
Pepper to taste

In a medium frying pan, brown chicken until done.

Cook noodles in water according to package directions and drain.

Heat butter and cream in a small saucepan over low heat until butter melts. Stir in remaining ingredients. Keep warm over low heat. Top warm noodles with chicken and sauce.

THAI CHICKEN

Makes 3–4 servings

4 cups water
2 packages chicken ramen noodles, with seasoning packets
½ cup shredded cooked chicken
1 carrot, thinly sliced with a vegetable peeler
½ cucumber, peeled, seeds removed, and thinly sliced
4 tablespoons spicy Thai peanut sauce

In a medium saucepan, bring water and 1 seasoning packet to a boil. Add noodles and cook for 3 minutes; drain. Toss noodles with remaining ingredients, adding more peanut sauce if needed until evenly coated, but not runny. Chill slightly or serve at room temperature.

FIESTA CHICKEN

Makes 2–4 servings

1 pound boneless, skinless chicken breasts, cut into chunks
Olive oil
½ cup corn
½ cup black beans, drained and rinsed
½ cup chopped red bell pepper
2 packages Cajun chicken ramen noodles, with seasoning packets
2–3 tablespoons sour cream
2 tablespoons salsa

In a large frying pan, brown chicken in olive oil. Add corn, black beans, and pepper. Sauté over low heat until heated through and vegetables are tender.

Cook noodles in water according to package directions and drain. Add seasoning packets. Combine noodles with chicken mixture. Stir in sour cream and salsa.

CHICKEN LO MEIN

Makes 2 servings

1 tablespoon vegetable oil
1 tablespoon soy sauce
1 pound boneless, skinless chicken breasts, cut into strips
$\frac{1}{2}$ cup sliced onion
$\frac{1}{2}$ cup chopped green bell pepper
$\frac{1}{4}$ cup chopped carrot
1 package chicken ramen noodles, with seasoning packet

In a large frying pan, mix oil, soy sauce, and half of the seasoning packet. Add chicken and brown until done. Add vegetables to chicken, and cook until tender.

Cook noodles in water according to package directions and drain. Add noodles to chicken and vegetables and cook over medium heat 3 minutes, stirring constantly.

CHILLED CAESAR CHICKEN

Makes 2–4 servings

4 cups water
2 packages ramen noodles, any flavor
¹/₂ cup Caesar salad dressing
2 boneless, skinless chicken breasts, cooked and diced
¹/₂ cup croutons
¹/₄ cup cooked and crumbled bacon

In a medium saucepan, bring water to a boil. Add noodles and cook for 2 minutes; drain. Add dressing and toss to coat. Allow to chill in refrigerator for 1 hour. Add remaining ingredients and toss.

TURKEY PASTA PIE

Makes 6 servings

¹/₂ **pound ground turkey**
¹/₄ **cup finely chopped onion**
1 **(14.5-ounce) can stewed tomatoes, with liquid**
1 **(8-ounce) can tomato sauce**
¹/₂ **teaspoon Italian seasoning**
6 **cups water**
3 **packages ramen noodles, any flavor**
2 **eggs, divided**
1 **tablespoon butter or margarine, melted**
1 **cup grated mozzarella cheese**
1 **cup creamy small-curd cottage cheese**
1 **(8-ounce) package frozen spinach, thawed and drained**
¹/₄ **cup grated Parmesan cheese**

Preheat oven to 350 degrees.

In a large frying pan, cook the turkey and onion over medium heat; drain. Stir in the tomatoes, tomato sauce, and Italian seasoning and bring to a boil; reduce heat. Cover and simmer for 10 minutes, stirring occasionally.

In a large saucepan, bring water to a boil. Add noodles and cook for 2 minutes; drain and set aside. Beat 1 egg and the butter in a large bowl. Add the noodles and mozzarella cheese; toss to mix. Place mixture into an ungreased 10-inch pie plate and press evenly on bottom and up side.

Mix the cottage cheese and remaining egg and then spread over the noodle mixture. Sprinkle with the spinach. Spoon turkey mixture evenly over top and then sprinkle with Parmesan cheese. Bake, uncovered, for 30 minutes, or until hot in center. Let stand 10 minutes before cutting.

PESTO TURKEY & PASTA

Makes 2–4 servings

4 cups water
2 packages ramen noodles, any flavor
2 cups diced cooked turkey breast
1/2 cup basil pesto
1/2 cup coarsely chopped roasted red bell peppers
Sliced black olives (optional)

In a medium saucepan, bring water to a boil. Add noodles and cook for 3 minutes; drain. Add the turkey, pesto, and bell peppers to the noodles. Heat over low heat, stirring constantly, until hot. Serve with a garnish of olives, if desired.

Seafood Mains

GARLIC SHRIMP 'N' VEGGIES

Makes 2–4 servings

1 green bell pepper, thinly sliced
1 red bell pepper, thinly sliced
1/2 small onion, thinly sliced
1 1/2 tablespoons minced garlic
3–4 tablespoons olive oil
2 cups cooked small shrimp, peeled and deveined
2 packages oriental ramen noodles, with seasoning packets

In a large frying pan, sauté peppers, onion, and garlic in oil until tender. Add shrimp and 1 seasoning packet. Simmer 3–5 minutes.

Cook noodles in water according to package directions and drain. Add half of remaining seasoning packet. Serve shrimp mixture over noodles.

SALMON SIMMER

Makes 2-4 servings

1 (14.5-ounce) can diced tomatoes, with liquid
2 (5-ounce) cans salmon, drained
2 tablespoons olive oil
2 packages vegetable ramen noodles, with seasoning packets
2 tablespoons oregano
2 tablespoons minced garlic
1 cup water
2 tablespoons grated Parmesan cheese

In a medium saucepan, combine the tomatoes, salmon, olive oil, seasoning packets, oregano, and garlic and bring to a simmer. Add the noodles and water. Cover and cook for 3 minutes. Serve sprinkled with Parmesan cheese.

CAJUN SHRIMP & CHICKEN GUMBO

2 cups water
Pinch of sugar
1 teaspoon butter or margarine
¼ teaspoon celery salt
1 teaspoon minced garlic
2 packages shrimp ramen noodles, with seasoning packets
1 (6-ounce) can shrimp, drained
1 chicken breast, cooked and cubed
¼ cup cooked and cubed Cajun sausage

In a medium saucepan, bring the water, sugar, butter, celery salt, garlic, and seasoning packets to a boil. Add the noodles, shrimp, chicken, and sausage. Cook for 3 minutes.

CRAB
LO MEIN

Makes 4–6 servings

5 ¼ cups water, divided
2 packages chicken ramen noodles, with seasoning packets
1 medium onion, julienned
1 medium green bell pepper, julienned
2 cups frozen broccoli cuts, thawed
¼ cup sliced fresh mushrooms
2 tablespoons canola oil
1 tablespoon cornstarch
¼ cup soy sauce
1 (12-ounce) can crab meat, lightly chopped

In a medium saucepan, bring 4 cups water to a boil. Add noodles and cook for 3 minutes; drain and set aside.

In a large frying pan over medium heat, sauté the onion, bell pepper, broccoli, and mushrooms in oil for 3–4 minutes or until tender-crisp.

In a small bowl, combine the cornstarch, remaining water, seasoning packets, and soy sauce. Gradually add to pan and cook over medium heat until thick, stirring constantly. Add crab and continue to cook for 2 minutes more. Add to the noodles and then toss and serve.

COCONUT CURRY SHRIMP

Makes 2-4 servings

4 cups water
2 packages ramen noodles, any flavor
1/2 cup coconut milk
1/3 cup creamy peanut butter
1 1/2 teaspoons curry
1 lime, juiced
1 pound large shrimp, cooked and cleaned
1/2 seedless cucumber, julienned
4 scallions, sliced

Bring water to a boil in a large frying pan. Add noodles and cover. Remove from heat and let stand 5 minutes.

Whisk the coconut milk, peanut butter, curry, and lime juice in a medium bowl to blend. Drain noodles and add shrimp, cucumber, scallions, and coconut milk mixture; toss to coat. Serve at room temperature.

TUNA NOODLE CASSEROLE

Makes 2–4 servings

2 (6-ounce) cans tuna, drained
1 cup grated cheddar cheese
$^1/_2$ cup water
1 cup milk
2 eggs, beaten
2 packages chicken ramen noodles, broken up and with seasoning packets
10–20 saltine crackers, crushed

Preheat oven to 350 degrees.

In a medium bowl, mix tuna, cheese, water, milk, eggs, and 1 seasoning packet. Transfer mixture to a casserole dish. Add broken uncooked noodles. Bake 15 minutes, stirring occasionally. Sprinkle crackers over top and bake 5 minutes more.

Veggie Mains
& Sides

SPINACH PARMESAN RAMEN

Makes 3–4 servings

4 ½ cups water, divided
2 packages vegetable ramen noodles, with seasoning packets
¼ cup chopped onion
1 teaspoon minced garlic
¼ cup frozen spinach, thawed and drained
4 tablespoons milk
1 tablespoon cream cheese
¼ cup grated Parmesan cheese
¼ cup grated mozzarella cheese

In a large saucepan, bring 4 cups water to a boil. Add noodles and cook 3 minutes; drain and set aside.

In a large saucepan, add remaining water and 1 seasoning packet, stirring until dissolved. Bring to a boil over medium heat. Add onion and garlic and let simmer for 5 minutes. Stir in spinach and cook for 2 minutes more. Add milk and cheeses, stirring until cheese is melted. Add noodles and toss until coated.

CHEESY VEGETABLE RAMEN

Makes 2 servings

1 package ramen noodles, any flavor, with seasoning packet
1 cup frozen mixed vegetables
1 tablespoon water
1 small jar creamy cheese sauce, condensed

Cook noodles in water according to package directions and drain. Add half of the seasoning packet and set aside.

In a medium frying pan, cook vegetables in water until tender. Add cheese sauce to vegetables and heat through. Stir in noodles.

PAN-FRIED NOODLES

Makes 2–4 servings

2 packages oriental ramen noodles, with seasoning packets
1 cup frozen peas and carrots
2 eggs
1–2 teaspoons oil
2–3 tablespoons soy sauce

Cook noodles in water according to package directions and drain. Add seasoning packets. Heat vegetables in microwave until heated through.

In a large frying pan, fry eggs in oil; break yolk and cook until hard, flipping occasionally. Cut eggs into pieces. Add noodles and vegetables to frying pan and toss to mix. Fry over medium-high heat about 3 minutes, turning frequently to prevent sticking. Sprinkle soy sauce over top and stir together, adding more if necessary.

ASIAN NOODLE TOSS

Makes 1-2 servings

2 cups water
1 package vegetable ramen noodles
4 baby carrots, julienned
¹/₂ cup sugar snap peas
1 (4-ounce) can mandarin oranges
1 tablespoon soy sauce
1 tablespoon orange jelly
1 tablespoon cider vinegar

In a small saucepan, bring water to a boil. Add noodles, carrots, and peas and cook for 3 minutes; drain and place in a bowl. Add the oranges, reserving the juice in a small bowl. To the juice, add the soy sauce, jelly, and vinegar; mix thoroughly. Drizzle over noodles, toss and serve warm.

GRILLED RAMEN

Makes 2–4 servings

1 package chicken, pork, or beef ramen noodles, with seasoning packet
2 tablespoons soy sauce
Dash of hot sauce
Dash of sesame oil
1 tablespoon marmalade
¼ cup hot water, not boiling

In a ziplock bag, combine the seasoning packet, soy sauce, hot sauce, sesame oil, marmalade, and hot water. Mix thoroughly. Add brick of noodles and seal completely. Tilt bag to allow marinade to coat the entire brick. Allow to sit for at least 15 minutes but no longer than 30 minutes. Flip occasionally to prevent marinade from pooling in one spot.

Over a medium flame, grill noodle brick for 3 minutes each side or until char marks appear. Be sure the brick is not stuck to the grill or it may pull apart when you try to flip or remove it. Serve with remaining marinade as "au jus" or place in a bowl and add 1 cup of boiling water for a less crunchy dish.

FRITTATAS

Makes 8 servings

2 cups water
1 package ramen noodles, any flavor, with seasoning packet
1 medium zucchini, shredded
2 scallions, cut into long, narrow strips
1 medium carrot, shredded
2 eggs, beaten
2 tablespoons flour
2 tablespoons vegetable oil, divided

In a small saucepan, bring water to a boil. Add noodles and let boil for 2 minutes; drain and place in a medium bowl. Stir in the zucchini, scallions, carrot, eggs, flour, and half of the seasoning packet.

Heat 1 tablespoon oil in a large nonstick frying pan over medium-high heat. Using half of the noodle mixture, make 4 pancakes. Fry 2–3 minutes per side. Repeat, using remaining oil. Serve as a side with entrees based on ramen flavor.

STUFFED TOMATOES

Makes 16 servings

8 large tomatoes
Dash of salt
1 cup water
1 package chicken or vegetable ramen noodles, crushed and with seasoning packet
½ pound sliced fresh mushrooms
2 tablespoons butter or margarine
1 tablespoon flour
½ cup half-and-half
2 tablespoons breadcrumbs
1 cup grated cheddar cheese, divided

Preheat oven to 400 degrees.

Cut tomatoes in half, scoop out pulp, and set aside. Sprinkle tomatoes with salt and invert on paper towels and let drain, about 15 minutes.

In a small saucepan, bring water to boil, add noodles, and let cook for 2 minutes; drain and set aside.

In a medium frying pan, sauté mushrooms in butter for 5 minutes. Add seasoning packet and flour; gradually stir in the half-and-half. Bring to a simmer stirring constantly until thick, about 2 minutes. Remove from heat and stir in breadcrumbs and ½ cup cheese. Add noodles and mix. Spoon into tomato cups and sprinkle with remaining cheese. Prepare two 9 x 13-inch baking dishes with nonstick cooking spray. Place tomatoes in dishes and bake, uncovered, for 10 minutes.

PIZZA PASTA

Makes 2–4 servings

2 packages ramen noodles, any flavor
2–3 cups spaghetti sauce
20–25 pepperoni slices, halved
³⁄₄ cup chopped green bell pepper
¹⁄₂ cup grated cheddar cheese
1 cup grated mozzarella cheese

Preheat oven to 350 degrees.

Cook noodles in water according to package directions and drain.

In a large saucepan, combine sauce, pepperoni, pepper, and cheddar cheese. Stir constantly until cheese is melted. Place noodles in a lightly greased 8 x 8-inch pan. Pour sauce mixture over top. Sprinkle with mozzarella cheese. Bake 15 minutes, or until cheese is melted.

CHEESY RANCH RAMEN

Makes 2–4 servings

2 packages finely chopped ramen noodles, any flavor
1 cup ranch dressing
2 cups grated cheddar cheese

Cook noodles in water according to package directions and drain. Add ranch dressing and cheese to noodles and cook over low heat, stirring constantly, until cheese is melted.

PRIMAVERA PASTA

Makes 2–4 servings

¼ cup slivered almonds
1 cup chopped broccoli
1 cup snow peas
1 cup sliced red bell pepper
½ cup thinly sliced carrots
½ cup thinly sliced red onion
3 tablespoons vegetable oil
2 packages chicken ramen noodles, broken up
1½ cups water

In a small frying pan, toast almonds until lightly browned and then set aside.

In a large frying pan or wok, stir-fry vegetables in oil 3–4 minutes. Add broken noodles and water. Steam 3–5 minutes, or until noodles are done, stirring occasionally. Top with almonds and serve.

BUTTERY CHIVE NOODLES

Makes 2–4 servings

2 packages ramen noodles, any flavor
2 tablespoons butter or margarine
¹/₂ cup chopped chives
Salt and pepper

Cook noodles in water according to package directions and drain. Add butter to warm noodles and stir until melted. Add chives and season to taste with salt and pepper.

Sweet on Ramen

TRAIL MIX

Makes 12 cups

3 packages ramen noodles, any flavor
15 small sticks beef jerky, cut into small pieces
½ pound dried apricots, cut into small pieces*
½ cup dried cranberries, blueberries, cherries, or bananas
2 cups dry roasted peanuts

Break noodles into a bowl. Add remaining ingredients and stir.

VARIATION: For a more traditional trail mix, omit the beef jerky and fruit. Add 1 pound plain M&Ms, 1 cup raisins, 1 cup sunflower seeds, and 3 cups granola cereal to broken up noodles and stir.

Any dried fruit combination may be substituted.

MAPLE & BROWN SUGAR RAMENMEAL

Makes 2 servings

1 package ramen noodles, any flavor
1 cup milk
1 tablespoon maple syrup
1 tablespoon brown sugar

Crumble ramen into a small microwave-safe bowl. Add milk, syrup, and sugar. Heat in the microwave on high for 4 minutes, stirring occasionally.

VARIATION: If you'd rather have something fruity, omit the syrup and sugar and add 1 banana, sliced, 1 cup of blueberries, or a mixture of ½ cup diced apples, 1 teaspoon cinnamon, and 1 tablespoon sugar.

CARAMEL CRISPS

Makes 10–15 servings

½ cup butter or margarine
½ cup brown sugar
⅛ teaspoon vanilla
1 tablespoon corn syrup
1 package ramen noodles, any flavor, finely crushed

Preheat oven to 300 degrees.

Liberally prepare a baking sheet with nonstick cooking spray.

In a small saucepan, mix the butter, brown sugar, vanilla, and corn syrup over medium heat until it starts to bubble and thicken, stirring often; remove from heat. Add noodles and toss to mix. Pour the mixture onto baking sheet and put in the oven for 4 minutes. Remove from the oven and cool in the fridge or freezer. Slice and serve.

THIN MINT ON A STICK

Makes 12

1 (8-ounce) bag dark chocolate chips
6 drops peppermint extract
1 drop spearmint extract
1 drop wintergreen extract
2 packages ramen noodles, any flavor, crushed
12 craft sticks

In a medium saucepan or double boiler, melt the chocolate chips until they become smooth and creamy. Slowly add extracts to the chocolate. Stir for 1 minute. Add noodles and stir vigorously until completely covered. Using a tablespoon, immediately spoon mixture onto wax paper in round cookie shapes. Mixture will flatten and spread considerably, so leave lots of space in between. Place craft stick in each and chill in refrigerator until solid, about 1 hour.

INDEX

A

Asian Noodle Toss, 108
Asparagus, Chicken 'n', 81

B

Bacon:
    Bacon-Fried Ramen, 72
    Breakfast Ramen, 71
    Cheesy Bacon Noodles, 59
    Chilled Caesar Chicken, 89
    Yatsobi, 41
Bean sprouts:
    Miso & Veggie Ramen Soup, 18
    Three Sprout Salad, 34
    Yatsobi, 41
Beans:
    Beefy Chili Noodles, 54
    Fiesta Chicken, 86
    South of the Border Ramen
        Soup, 17
    Polish Ramen Salad, 36
    Spicy Shrimp & Noodle Soup,
        14
Beef ramen noodles:
    Beef & Broccoli Stir-Fry, 51
    Beef & Chestnut Casserole, 53
    Beef Provençale, 47
    Beef Sukiyaki, 52
    Beefy Chili Noodles, 54
    Beefy Mushroom Noodles, 49
    Cheddar Beef Casserole, 48
    Cheeseburger Ramen, 56
    Creamy Beef & Broccoli
        Noodles, 46
    Grilled Ramen, 110
    Ramen Rolled Steak, 38
    Slow Cooker Beef & Noodles, 42
    Stuffed Bell Peppers, 44
    Taco Salad, 26

Beef:
    Beef & Broccoli Stir-Fry, 51
    Beef & Chestnut Casserole, 53
    Beef Provençale 47
    Beef Ramenoff, 43
    Beef Sukiyaki, 52
    Beefy Chili Noodles, 54
    Beefy Mushroom Noodles, 49
    Cheddar Beef Casserole, 48
    Cheeseburger Ramen, 56
    Creamy Beef & Broccoli
        Noodles, 46
    Ramen Rolled Steak, 38
    Slow Cooker Beef & Noodles, 42
    Stuffed Bell Peppers, 44
    Taco Salad, 26
    Yatsobi, 41
Bell pepper(s):
    Chicken Fajita Ramen Salad, 33
    Chicken Lo Mein, 88
    Crab Lo Mein, 98
    Fiesta Chicken, 86
    Garlic Shrimp 'n' Veggies, 95
    Honey Grilled Chicken, 83
    Pesto Turkey & Pasta, 92
    Pizza Pasta, 114
    Primavera Pasta, 116
    Saucy Chops & 62
    Spicy Sausage Ramen, 67
    Stuffed Bell Peppers, 44
    Tofu & Cabbage Toss, 29
    Yatsobi, 41
Black-Eyed Peas & Ham, 13
Breakfast Ramen, 71
Broccoli:
    Beef & Broccoli Stir-Fry, 51
    Broccoli, Mushroom, & Ham
        Casserole, 66
    Cheesy Chicken Divan, 76

Chicken Broccoli Bake, 75
Creamy Beef & Broccoli
    Noodles, 46
Honey Grilled Chicken, 83
Nutty Broccoli Slaw, 25
Primavera Pasta, 116

C

Cabbage:
    Miso & Veggie Ramen Soup, 18
    Oriental Chicken Salad, 28
    Tangerine Chicken Salad, 30
    Tofu & Cabbage Toss, 29
    Yatsobi, 41
Carrot(s):
    Frittatas, 111
    Herbed Chicken, 77
    Honey Grilled Chicken, 83
    Pan-Fried Noodles, 107
    Primavera Pasta, 116
    Tangerine Chicken Salad, 30
    Yatsobi, 41
Casseroles:
    Beef & Chestnut, 53
    Broccoli, Mushroom, & Ham, 66
    Cheddar Beef, 48
    Cheesy Chicken Divan, 76
    Cheesy Chicken, 80
    Chicken Broccoli Bake, 75
    Pizza Pasta, 114
    Tuna Noodle, 102
Cheeseburger Ramen, 56
Cheesy Chicken Casserole, 80
Cheesy Chicken Divan, 76
Cheesy Ranch Ramen, 115
Cheesy Vegetable Ramen, 106
Chicken:
    Cajun Shrimp & Chicken
        Gumbo, 97

Cheesy Chicken Casserole, 80
Cheesy Chicken Divan, 76
Chicken Alfredo, 84
Chicken Fajita Ramen Salad, 33
Chicken Lo Mein, 88
Chicken 'n' Asparagus, 81
Chilled Caesar Chicken, 89
Curried Chicken Soup, 12
Fiesta Chicken, 86
Herbed Chicken, 77
Honey Grilled Chicken, 83
Hot & Sour Ramen, 78
Oriental Chicken Salad, 28
Quick Chicken Salad, 27
Slow Chicken Soup, 11
South of the Border Ramen Soup, 17
Tangerine Chicken Salad, 30
Thai Chicken, 85
Chicken ramen noodles:
    Breakfast Ramen, 71
    Broccoli, Mushroom, & Ham Casserole, 66
    Cheesy Chicken Casserole, 80
    Cheesy Chicken Divan, 76
    Chicken Broccoli Bake, 75
    Chicken Lo Mein, 88
    Chicken 'n' Asparagus, 81
    Chunky Noodle Salad, 19
    Crab Lo Mein, 98
    Curried Chicken Soup, 12
    Fiesta Chicken, 86
    Gingered Pork & Snow Peas, 68
    Grilled Ramen, 110
    Herbed Chicken, 77
    Miso & Veggie Ramen Soup, 18
    Nutty Broccoli Slaw, 25
    Polish Ramen Salad, 36
    Primavera Pasta, 116
    Quick Chicken Salad, 27
    Slow Chicken Soup, 11

South of the Border Ramen Soup, 17
Stuffed Tomatoes, 113
Tangerine Chicken Salad, 30
Thai Chicken, 85
Tuna Noodle Casserole, 102
Chive Noodles, Buttery, 118
Coconut Curry Shrimp, 101
Crab Lo Mein, 98

H

Ham & Black-Eyed Peas, 13
Ham, in Tropical Ramen, 65
Hot Dogs, Oriental, 57

M

Mandarin Salad, Tossed, 20
Mushroom(s):
    Beef Provençale, 47
    Beef Sukiyaki, 52
    Beefy Mushroom Noodles, 49
    Broccoli, Mushroom, & Ham Casserole, 66
    Crab Lo Mein, 98
    Stuffed Tomatoes, 113

O

Oriental ramen noodles:
    Garlic Shrimp 'n' Veggies, 95
    Hot & Sour Ramen, 78
    Oriental Chicken Salad, 28
    Oriental Hot Dogs, 57
    Pan-Fried Noodles, 107
    Spicy Shrimp & Noodle Soup, 14

P

Parmesan Ramen, Spinach, 105
Peas:
    Asian Noodle Toss, 108
    Pan-Fried Noodles, 107
    Primavera Pasta, 116
Pesto Turkey & Pasta, 92

Pork:
    Cajun Shrimp & Chicken Gumbo, 97
    Gingered Pork & Snow Peas, 68
    Hungarian Goulash à la Ramen, 61
    Miso & Veggie Ramen Soup, 18
    Pork Chops & Ramen, 60
    Saucy Chops & Peppers, 62
    Spicy Sausage Ramen, 67
Pork ramen noodles:
    Grilled Ramen, 110
    Ham & Black-Eyed Peas, 13
    Pork Chops & Ramen, 60
    Saucy Chops & Peppers, 62
Primavera Pasta, 116

R

Ramen noodles, any flavor:
    Antipasto Salad, 23
    Bacon-Fried Ramen, 72
    Beef Ramenoff, 43
    Buttery Chive Noodles, 118
    Caramel Crisps, 123
    Cheesy Bacon Noodles, 59
    Cheesy Ranch Ramen, 115
    Cheesy Vegetable Ramen, 106
    Chicken Alfredo, 84
    Chilled Caesar Chicken, 89
    Coconut Curry Shrimp, 101
    Crunchy Fruit Salad, 22
    Frittatas, 111
    Honey Grilled Chicken, 83
    Hungarian Goulash à la Ramen, 61
    Maple & Brown Sugar Ramenmeal, 122
    Pesto Turkey & Pasta, 92
    Pizza Pasta, 114
    Thin Mint on a Stick, 124
    Three Sprout Salad, 34
    Tofu & Cabbage Toss, 29
    Tossed Mandarin Salad, 20

Trail Mix, 121
Tropical Ramen, 65
Turkey Pasta Pie, 90
Yatsobi, 41

S
Salads:
 Antipasto, 23
 Chicken Fajita Ramen, 33
 Chunky Noodle, 19
 Crunchy Fruit, 22
 Nutty Broccoli Slaw, 25
 Oriental Chicken, 28
 Polish Ramen, 36
 Quick Chicken, 27
 Taco, 26
 Tangerine Chicken, 30
 Three Sprout Salad, 34
 Tofu & Cabbage Toss, 29
 Tossed Mandarin, 20
Salmon Simmer, 96
Shrimp:
 Cajun Shrimp & Chicken
  Gumbo, 97
 Coconut Curry Shrimp, 101
 Garlic Shrimp 'n' Veggies, 95
 Spicy Shrimp & Noodle Soup, 14
Soups:
 Curried Chicken, 12
 Ham & Black-Eyed Peas, 13
 Miso & Veggie Ramen, 18
 Slow Chicken, 11
 South of the Border Ramen, 17
 Spicy Shrimp & Noodle, 14
Spicy ramen noodles: Chicken
 Fajita Ramen Salad, 33
Spinach:
 Beef Sukiyaki, 52
 Spinach Parmesan Ramen, 105

Turkey Pasta Pie, 90
Sweets:
 Caramel Crisps, 123
 Maple & Brown Sugar
  Ramenmeal, 122
 Thin Mint on a Stick, 124
 Trail Mix, 121

T
Tangerine Chicken Salad, 30
Tofu & Cabbage Toss, 29
Tomato(es):
 Beef Provençale, 47
 Beefy Chili Noodles, 54
 Cheeseburger Ramen, 56
 Polish Ramen Salad, 36
 Salmon Simmer, 96
 Spicy Sausage Ramen, 67
 Stuffed Bell Peppers, 44
 Stuffed Tomatoes, 113
 Turkey Pasta Pie, 90
Trail Mix, 121

Tuna Noodle Casserole, 102
Turkey & Pasta, Pesto, 92
Turkey Pasta Pie, 90
Turkey, smoked breast, in Chunky
 Noodle Salad, 19

V
Vegetable ramen noodles:
 Asian Noodle Toss, 108
 Curried Chicken Soup, 12
 Salmon Simmer, 96
 Spinach Parmesan Ramen, 105
 Stuffed Tomatoes, 113
Vegetable Ramen, Cheesy, 106

W
Water chestnuts, in Beef &
 Chestnut Casserole, 53

Z
Zucchini, in Frittatas, 111
Zucchini, in Oriental Hot Dogs, 57

METRIC CONVERSION CHART

VOLUME MEASUREMENTS		WEIGHT MEASUREMENTS		TEMPERATURE CONVERSION	
U.S.	Metric	U.S.	Metric	Fahrenheit	Celsius
1 teaspoon	5 ml	½ ounce	15 g	250	120
1 tablespoon	15 ml	1 ounce	30 g	300	150
¼ cup	60 ml	3 ounces	90 g	325	160
⅓ cup	75 ml	4 ounces	115 g	350	180
½ cup	125 ml	8 ounces	225 g	375	190
⅔ cup	150 ml	12 ounces	350 g	400	200
¾ cup	175 ml	1 pound	450 g	425	220
1 cup	250 ml	2¼ pounds	1 kg	450	230